Colonial American Activity Book

Author   Linda Milliken
Illustrator   Barb Lorseyedi

Table of Contents

METRIC CONVERSION CHART

Refer to this chart when metric conversions are not found within the activity.

4 tsp	=	1 ml	4 cup	=	60 ml	350° F =	180° C	1 inch	=	2.54 cm
2 tsp	=	2 ml	3 cup	=	80 ml	375° F =	190° C	1 foot	=	30 cm
1 tsp	=	5 ml	2 cup	=	125 ml	400° F =	200° C	1 yard	=	91 cm
1 Tbsp	=	15 ml	1 cup	=	250 ml	425° F =	216° C	1 mile	=	1.6 km
			1 oz.	=	28 g				
			1 lb.	=	.45 kg				

EP003 • ©1996 Edupress, Inc. • P.O. Box 883 • Dana Point, CA 92629
www.edupressinc.com
ISBN 1-56472-003-9
Printed in USA

Aboard the Mayflower

HISTORICAL AID:

The ship that carried 102 Pilgrims to America in 1620 was called the *Mayflower.* The exact size of the ship is not known but was probably about 90 feet long and 25 feet wide. There was a main deck, a gun deck, and areas for the captain, crew and passengers to eat and sleep.

The voyage, which began on September 16, 1620, took 66 days. It was not an easy trip as high winds and stormy seas took a toll on both ship and people. Crowded conditions also made travel uncomfortable. When land was finally sighted, the travellers were overjoyed—not only because a new life was beginning, but because the voyage across the Atlantic was over!

Projects:

On the Mayflower

Reproduce the drawing of the *Mayflower* on the following page. Color people and cargo on the ship. Cut out and paste to blue construction paper.

Chart a Voyage

Measure a length of 22 feet on a classroom wall. At one end write *England.* At the other end write *America.* Starting in England, tack a ship (use the pattern on the next page) to the wall. Measure and move the ship forward 4″ each day. Mark the days on a large calendar posted on the wall. At the end of 66 days, the front of the ship will arrive in "America!"

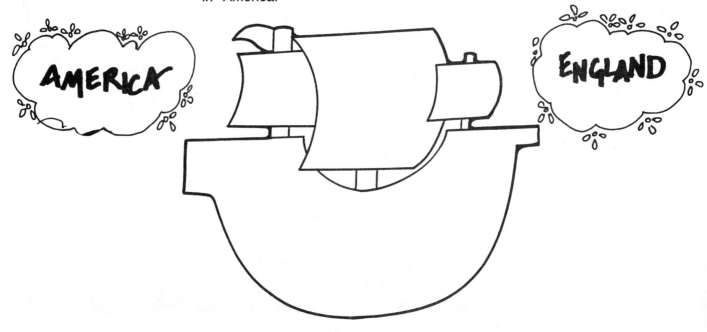

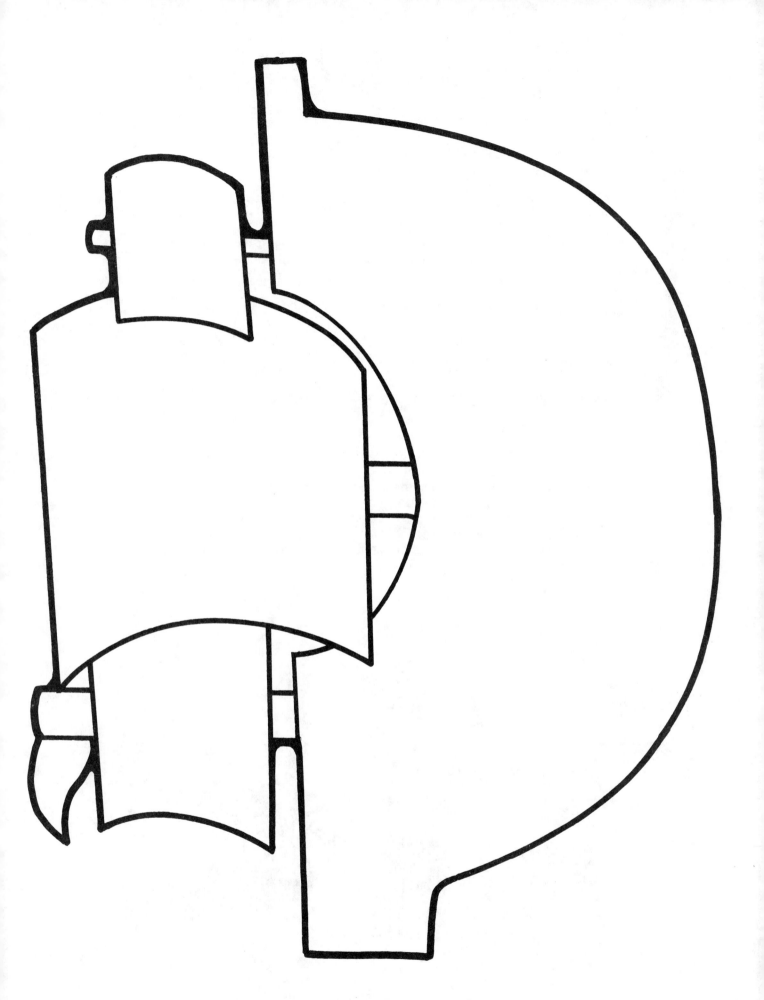

Mayflower Compact

HISTORICAL AID:

When the Pilgrims aboard the Mayflower first landed in America they knew they would need discipline among themselves. The leaders persuaded 41 male adults to sign the *Mayflower Compact*. This document set up the first form of government in Plymouth Colony. John Carver was elected governor. The others who signed were freemen who met once a year in a General Court to discuss the problems of the colony.

Although the original document has disappeared the compact on the following page has similar language.

Materials:

Make a classroom compact using the form on the next page.
- Fill in all the missing information.
- Unlike the original Mayflower Compact all members of the class will sign.
- Discuss and vote on the rules for your classroom colony.
- Meet once a month to discuss problems, alter rules and elect a new governor.

Classroom Compact

Whose names are underwritten, the loyal subjects of ye teacher

_____, of our school _____
　　　　　　　(teacher's name)　　　　　　　　　　　　　　　　　　(name of school)

Haveing undertaken ye advancement of education, do by these presents solimnly
& mutualy in ye presence of ye teacher and one of another, covenant, & combine
ourselves togeather into a Civill body politick; for our better ordering, &
preservation & furtherance of ye ends aforesaid; and by vertue hereof to enacte,
constitute, and frame such just & equall Lawes, ordinances, Acts, constitutions &
offices, from time to time, as shall be thought most   mete & convenients for ye
generall good of ye classroom: unto which we promise all due submission and
obedience. In witness whereof we have hereunder subscribed our names at

_____ ye _____ of _____ in ye year of
　　　　　(city)　　　　　　　　(day)　　　　　(month)

_____.
　(year)

Pilgrim Clothing

HISTORICAL AID

Pilgrims dressed like people of the same class in England. They wore simple but colorful clothes. For the first few years in Plymouth colony there was no flax grown. This flax was needed to make linen for clothing. The women had to constantly mend and patch the threadbare garments they had brought with them from England. There were no special clothes for children. They wore outfits of the same color and style as their parents.

Pilgrim men and boys wore full breeches to the knee in colors of gray, brown, tan, blue or rusty red. Knit stockings came up to their hips. Sleeveless leather vest jackets, called *jerkins,* were worn over white linen shirts. On their heads they wore either wool stocking caps or wide brim hats with a low crown.

Pilgrim women and girls wore bright colors of red, purple, blue or green. Their skirts were full and reached to their ankles. Covering the skirt was an apron. A Pilgrim woman would have been embarrassed to be seen in public without her apron! A hood was worn beneath a high crowned hat and a white cloth was wrapped around the neck and shoulders.

Have a Pilgrim dress-up day!
Follow the suggestions on this and the next page.

Boys

Cut collars from white construction paper (see illustration).

Cut vests from brown butcher paper (see illustration).

Roll pants to the knees and wear long white socks.

Wear a white, long-sleeved shirt under the vest.

Wear a stocking cap. If a cap isn't available, cut a sock in half.

Girls

Make aprons from white butcher paper (see illustration).

Wear a long, colorful skirt. (Borrow one from mom.)

Tie a white cloth scarf around the head. Wrap the neck with white cloth and pin in the front (see illustration).

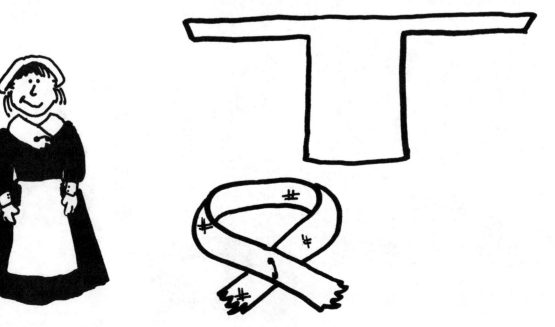

Homelife

HISTORICAL AID:

Furnishings of the early colonial settlers were usually homemade—plain and strong. Thick wooden planks served as tables. Blocks of wood, small barrels or rough benches were used as chairs. Mattresses were canvas bags stuffed with straw and placed on the floor.

More wealthy colonists had finer furniture. Some came from England. Others were copied by colonial craftsmen. They used cherry, maple, pine and walnut in the building of tables, chairs, dressers (called highboys and lowboys), tall cupboards and four poster beds.

The most famous colonial clock was called a grandfather clock. It had a tall wooden case and stood on the floor. Other furnishings included candlesticks, chandeliers and mirrors.

There were no closets. Clothes not in a dresser hung from pegs in the walls.

Cooking was done in a large fireplace which also provided light and heat. At mealtime the men and older boys sat with their hats on. If a daughter was old enough to serve, the wife sat next to her husband. Younger children stood in absolute silence and ate what was given to them. Some ate standing at a separate table. *All* ate with their fingers. Clean linen napkins were used at every meal.

Classroom Project:
Set up a colonial home in your classroom. Use the suggestions on the following page for furnishings and activities. Encourage children to contribute items from home.

Furnishings

Fireplace

Tack rectangular construction paper bricks to the wall. Leave an opening in the center. Cut a large black kettle from butcher paper and "hang" it in the opening. Color and cut utensils (ladles, spoons) to hang along the hearth.

Grandfather Clock

Sketch and paint a replica of a grandfather clock. Tack it to the wall.

Mattresses

Stuff old pillowcases or burlap sacks with newspaper strips.

Tables & Chairs

Set plywood on two sawhorses. Use small barrels, ice cream cartons and blocks of wood or masonry for chairs. Set candles in candlesticks on the table. (For decoration only!)

Activities

- Pretend to cook and sleep in your colonial home. Nap or read on the mattresses. "Huddle" around the fireplace for warmth.

- Eat lunch at the table. Choose someone to be the head of the family. Remember—children stand silently at the table. Select 2 ladies to help serve. Bring in cloth scraps for napkins. Fingers only!

- Make a rag rug (see page 27) for the floor.

Plymouth Rock

HISTORICAL AID

According to popular story, the Pilgrims on the *Mayflower* stepped ashore on a large rock when they landed in America on December 21, 1620. Historians believe this rock was nearby when the Pilgrims landed and it has become a very famous American landmark. The granite boulder has the date of the landing inscribed on it and is placed near the Plymouth waterfront in a pit protected with an iron railing.

Project:

Make Plymouth Rock from papier-mache. You can buy this mix in variety or craft stores. Wallpaper paste also works well.

Tear **sheets of newspaper** into narrow strips about one-inch wide. Cover the strips with paste by pulling each strip through the paste. Or, spread the paste on each strip with a paintbrush. Cover a **shoebox** with these strips. Lay strips in one direction, then lay strips in the other direction so that they go across the first layer. Smooth down. Continue until you have put on about six layers.

Dry the projects in an open place for two or more days. When dry, paint gray. When the gray paint has dried, paint '1620' with black paint.

Jamestown Home

Project—home replica:
Cut a "chimney" hole in the center of the bottom of a shoe box and an opening in one side for a door. Glue weeds to the top. Glue popsicle sticks vertically and small twigs and stems horizontally to the sides. Paint brown or spread with a thin mud mixture.

Oiled Paper Windows

HISTORICAL AID:

Glass windows were a luxury the early colonial settlers could not have. As homes were built, window coverings had to be invented that would let in light but keep out some of the harsh weather.

One solution was to cover heavy parchment with oil. The oil served as waterproofing for the parchment which was nailed to the window opening.

Activity:

Cover a piece of butcher paper with salad oil. The children can take turns rubbing in the oil with the palm of their hand. (Have a supply of paper towels ready for cleaning oily hands.)

Experiment with the oiled paper:

- Take it outside. Does the sun shine through?
- Turn off the classroom lights and shine a flashlight through. What do you see?
- Spray water on it. What happens?
- Turn a fan on and stand behind the paper. Do you feel the wind?

What other experiments can you think of?

Squanto—Planting a Garden

HISTORICAL AID

Squanto (also called *Tisquantum*) was a Patuxet Indian who befriended the Pilgrims and helped them survive at Plymouth Colony. Squanto had been kidnapped by fishermen and lived in England for several years where he learned to speak English. After he returned home to America he met the Pilgrims. They had angered the Wamapanoag Indians by stealing corn, and they were nearly starving after their first difficult winter.

Squanto arranged a peace treaty between the Pilgrims and the Indians. He introduced them to the maize (corn) that became their means to survival. Squanto also taught them which wild berries and herbs to eat, how to fish and how to trade with the Indians for pelts. He showed the Pilgrims the best way to plant their crops. Three or four kernels of corn were planted in hills with fish for fertilizer. Squash was planted among the corn and bean vines climbed the cornstalks.

Without Squanto's help and guidance it is doubtful the Pilgrims would have survived in Plymouth Colony.

Classroom Project:

"Plant" a Wall Garden

Attach butcher paper to the wall, low enough so that children can reach to work. Glue a garden to the wall. You can use corn husks, yarn and raffia for vines and stalks, construction paper for beans, corn and pumpkins (don't forget the fish!), real leaves from home gardens, and seed samples from the market. Use the illustration as a guide.

Thanksgiving

HISTORICAL AID:

For the Pilgrims the first winter in the colonies was a harsh one. Half of the group died and, for a while, it looked as if no one would survive. So in the autumn of 1621, when a bumper crop of corn was harvested, it was decided a celebration was in order. Ninety Indians joined the Pilgrims for three days of feasting and merrymaking.

Hunting groups returned with deer and fowl. Turkeys, venison and deer were roasted. Fish, clams, oysters, lobsters, corn, pumpkins, beans and squash were also eaten.

Games were a part of the celebration. Men showed their skill with guns and bow and arrow. There were races, wrestling matches, singing and dancing.

A year later the food crop was less abundant and new arrivals to the colony created a food shortage. By the third spring in 1623 excessive heat caused crops to dry up. A day of fasting and prayer was ordered by the governor. Soon thereafter came a long rain. To celebrate, the governor proclaimed November 29 of that year a day of thanksgiving. Some feel that this festival rather than the one in 1621 was the true beginning of our present Thanksgiving Day.

In the following years thanksgiving festivals would be held whenever there was a reason to celebrate and be thankful. It wasn't until the end of the Civil War that President Abraham Lincoln proclaimed the last Thursday in November as Thanksgiving Day for the whole nation.

Project:

Celebrate Thanksgiving in your classroom. Use the suggestions on the following page to help you in your planning.

Thanksgiving Celebration

Costumes

Dress half the group as Pilgrims (see clothing directions pages 6-7).

Dress the other half as Indians. Make a simple feather headband for both boys and girls. Tuck paper into the waistband of pants for boys' loincloth. Fringe brown butcher paper and wrap around girls for a skirt.

Food

Follow any of the recipes for corn or pumpkins (pages 16-19). Sample green beans, squash and sliced turkey. Make popcorn.

Games and Activities

- **Stone's Throw**—Throw stones at a target chalked on the ground. The closest to the center wins.

- **Turkey Hunt**—Hunt for hidden paper turkeys. Or divide into two teams—the turkeys hide and the hunters look for them.

- **Husk or Bust**—Have a corn husking contest.

- **Spoonball**—This is an early form of croquet. Use a broom as a club and hit a small rubber ball or golf ball through a wire hoop.

- **Rhythm fun**—Dance to the beat of drums played by the Indians.

Bartering With Corn

Class Project:

Ask children to bring unwanted items to class for a "yard sale." Price the items—but, instead of pricing in dollars and cents, charge kernels of popped corn. The class can work together to determine the cost of the items. This will be an interesting lesson in money for younger students. Older children will learn about supply and demand. On the day of the sale, pop corn and pass out an equal number of kernels to each child. Be sure to supply ziplock baggies for the popcorn. After the sale, eat your profits!

Cook Up Some Corn

HISTORICAL AID

Corn became a basic food in every colonial household. Methods for grinding and cooking were all learned from the Indians. Corn was roasted in its own husk, boiled into a porridge called *samp*, and cooked with beans into a mixture called *succotash*. The most common cooked form was cornbread. Cornmeal was mixed with water or milk, salt and lard and shaped into buns. This mixture was fried on a hoe or griddle or in the ashes of the fireplace. Cornbread had different names in various parts of colonial America. It was also called *ashcake*, *hoecake*, *johnny cake* or *corn pone*.

Cornbread

Mix **1 cup cornmeal** with **1 teaspoon salt**. Add **½ cup milk** and **1 teaspoon cooking oil**.

Drop by the spoonful into a frying pan of hot oil. Brown on both sides.

Serve with butter. (Makes 12-15 corncakes.)

Pumpkin Potluck

HISTORICAL AID:

Pumpkins are an old-fashioned treat going back to American history before the landing of the Pilgrims. The Indians taught the early colonists how to plant and harvest this food. The colonists created different recipes and ways to serve this treat.

Early American housewives learned to split pumpkins, remove the seeds, put the halves back together and roast the whole pumpkins in hearth ovens.

Pumpkins were also boiled, cut in chunks and eaten salted and buttered. Pulp was mashed to make soup, bread dough, pudding, cakes and pies.

Although these recipes can be made using canned pumpkin, children would gain a better understanding of colonial life if they made their own pumpkin purée.

Boiled:
Slice open the pumpkin. Clean out seeds and membrane. Cut pumpkin into pieces, place in a large pot. Cover pumpkin pieces with water and cook until tender. Drain and peel outer skin. Mash pulp with wooden spoons.

Baked:
Slice pumpkin in half and clean out seeds and membrane. Put halves cut-side down in a baking dish. Bake in a 325° oven 45 minutes. Peel outer skin and mash pulp with a wooden spoon.

Roasted Pumpkin Seeds

Rinse seeds and blot dry with paper towel. Spread evenly on an ungreased cookie sheet. Bake in 375° oven for 12-15 minutes until crisp and slightly brown. Salt to taste.

Pumpkin Soup

6 cups cooked pumpkin
6 cups chicken broth
2 Tbs. butter

2 Tbs. flour
4 Tbs. brown sugar
1 tsp. cinnamon

Mix pumpkin and chicken broth. Blend in flour and butter. Add remaining ingredients. Heat (do not boil). Makes 24 ¼-cup servings.

Pumpkin-Nut Casserole

6 cups cooked pumpkin
⅔ cup butter
½ cup light cream
4 Tbs. brown sugar

1 tsp. salt
½ tsp. pepper
½ tsp. cinnamon
½ tsp. nutmeg

Mix all ingredients. Pour into buttered 3-quart casserole. Top with ground nuts. Bake 45 minutes at 350°.

Pumpkin Bread

2 cups flour
1 tsp. baking soda
1 tsp. salt
1 tsp. pumpkin pie spice
1½ cups sugar

½ cup vegetable oil
2 eggs, beaten
1 cup cooked pumpkin
¼ cup water

Sift together dry ingredients. Blend sugar, oil, eggs and pumpkin, and add to dry ingredients. Beat well. Pour into greased, floured loaf pan and bake in 350° oven 1 hour and 10 minutes.

Pumpkin Pie

2 cups cooked pumpkin
¾ cup sugar
2 tsp. cinnamon
½ tsp. nutmeg
¼ tsp. ground cloves

3 eggs, slightly beaten
1 cup light cream
1 nine-inch unbaked pie shell
½ tsp. salt

Blend pumpkin, sugar, spices and salt. Then blend in eggs and cream. Pour into pie shell. Bake 40-50 minutes (until knife inserted comes out clean) in 400° oven.

An Apple a Day

The colonists brought both apple seeds and trees from England to their new home. Twenty years after settling, fruit orchards were flourishing. Colonial cooks put the abundant apple crops to good use making tarts, pies, sauce, butter and cider.

Apples were also strung with linen thread and hung on walls to dry. Dried apples were eaten and used to make dolls.

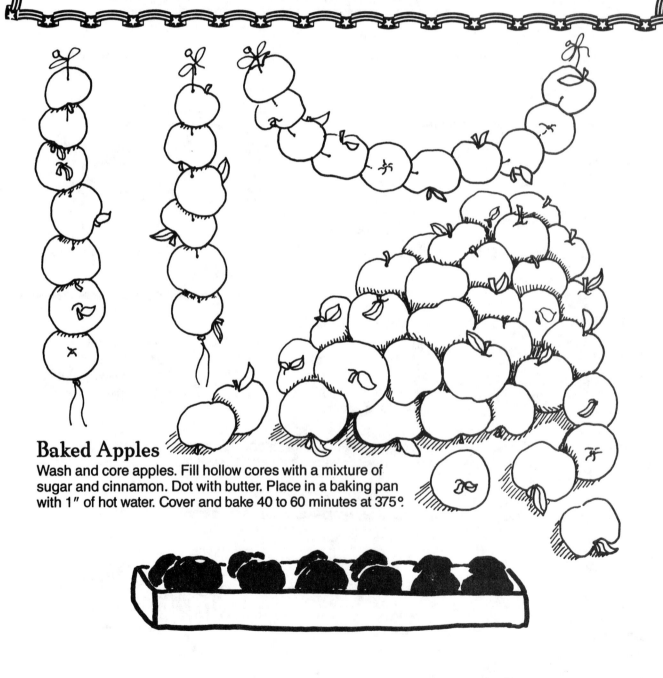

Baked Apples

Wash and core apples. Fill hollow cores with a mixture of sugar and cinnamon. Dot with butter. Place in a baking pan with 1″ of hot water. Cover and bake 40 to 60 minutes at 375°.

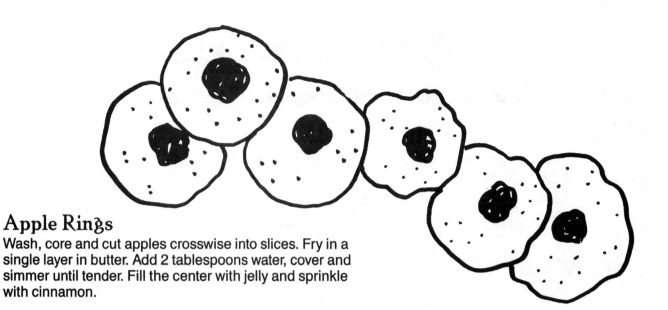

Apple Rings

Wash, core and cut apples crosswise into slices. Fry in a single layer in butter. Add 2 tablespoons water, cover and simmer until tender. Fill the center with jelly and sprinkle with cinnamon.

Apple Butter

2½ lbs. green apples
apple cider
1½ cups sugar
2 tablespoons butter

Remove stem from apples; cut in thick slices. Place in a pan and cover apples with cider. Bring to boil and cook 20 minutes or until soft. Press through a sieve. Stir in sugar, bring to a boil. Reduce heat, continue to cook and stir mixture until thick, about 20 minutes. Add butter. Cook until mixture leaves sides of pan, about 20 minutes. Serve on graham crackers or cornbread.

Yield: 4 cups

Digging For Clams

HISTORICAL AID

Among the many things that Squanto taught the Pilgrims was the skill of fishing. He taught them to catch shellfish and to spear fish. He also showed them how to dig in the sand for clams. All of these skills were new to the Pilgrims and helped them to survive during the early years of their settlement.

Dig for clams in your classroom!

Buy three or four clams at a local seafood store or market. Put several inches of sand in a shallow tub. Bury the clams in the tub. Add a few inches of water. How fast can each child find the buried clamshell? Spray a clamshell gold for the winner's "trophy."

After the contest, open the clams and show the children the meat inside.

Tea for Two!

HISTORICAL AID:

Can you guess what was the most popular colonial drink? For many it was tea. Hot chocolate, coffee, beer and cider were other drinks the colonists enjoyed.

For many years there was no tea so when it became available the colonists were not quite sure what to do with the leaves. Out of ignorance they put tea into water, boiled it, threw the liquid away and ate the leaves. In Salem, butter and salt were put on the leaves to improve the taste.

But for those who knew the correct preparation the choices were abundant. Many herbs and leaves were used to brew tea including raspberry, currant and sage leaves.

Have a tea sampling party!
Ask each child to bring a different type of *herbal* tea. Brew and sample. Provide simple biscuit cookies to be enjoyed with the tea.

Sweet Treats

Make *sucket* in your classroom!

Candied Citrus Peel
2 large grapefruit or
4 large oranges
  Water
1 cup sugar
  Cinnamon stick
6 cloves

Remove the peel from the fruit. Place in a medium saucepan. Cover with water and bring to a boil. Cook uncovered over medium heat for 20 minutes. Drain, rinse, cover with cold water and boil over medium heat until tender, about 15 minutes. Drain. Remove the white membrane by gently scraping with a spoon. Cut into ¼" wide strips.

In a medium sauce pan, combine 1 cup water, 1 cup sugar and spices. Bring to a boil stirring until sugar is dissolved. Add peel and cook over medium heat, stirring occasionally, until most of the syrup is absorbed. Drain well. Remove spices. Toss peel in ¾ cup sugar until coated.

Makes 2 cups orange peel or 3 cups grapefruit peel.

Town Crier

Activity:
Each day pick a different student to be the town crier. This child will be responsible for relating information to classmates. This could be as simple as announcing that it is recess or snack time or as advanced as reading assignment instructions and school bulletins.

Postal Service

HISTORICAL AID:

The first indication of an official postal system was in 1639 when the Massachusetts colony gave Richard Fairbanks permission to receive and dispatch mail from his home in Boston. He was paid one cent for each letter he handled. Letters and messages were carried by *postriders*—the first colonial mailmen. The postriders travelled a route called a *post road*. On the way they picked up news and letters and passed them on to the town criers. Letters were addressed by using descriptions, as there was no system of numbered addresses yet in existence. For example, a letter might be addressed to John Carpenter, house near the lumber mill, Boston, Massachusetts.

The United States Postal Service was officially begun in 1753. Benjamin Franklin was the first postmaster general.

Project:

Grades K-2—Mark a post road on the playground using chalk or yarn. Pretend you are a postrider delivering a message to a town crier. Carry an envelope down the post road and hand it to someone waiting at the other end.

Grades 3-6—Make up an address for your house. Remember, it cannot include numbers. It can include your street name. Think of the landmarks nearby that could help with your description. Count how many houses you are from the corner.

Rag Rug

HISTORICAL AID:
The floor of a colonial home was usually constructed with wooden planks which the women scrubbed and swept to keep clean. Sometimes they made rugs to cover portions of the floor. Material scraps were tied end to end, twisted, coiled into an oval or circle and sewn into position.

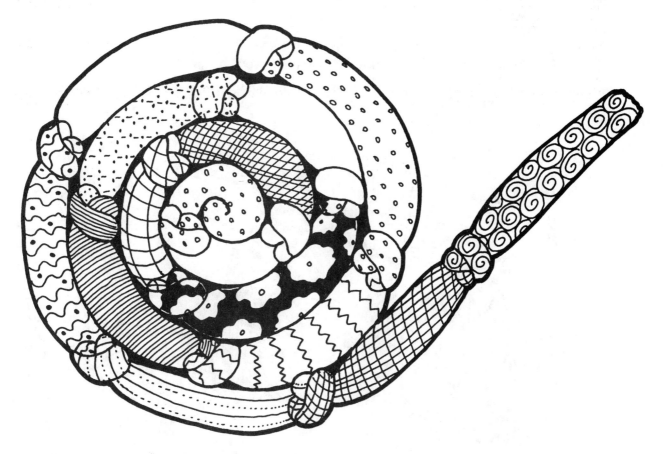

Project:
Ask children to bring strips of material scraps from home. Tie the strips end to end. (Each child can be responsible for tying the strips he or she brought.)

When the length of the tied strips is at least 50 feet begin to coil the material from one end. As the material is coiled children can spread glue to hold it in place. When the coiling is complete, mount the finished shape on cardboard for sturdiness.

Use the rug on your classroom floor or hang it on the wall as a display.

Feather Art

Project:

- Ask each child to bring in an old hat. If this is not possible check a local paint store for paper paint hats. They are either free or very inexpensive.

- Decorate each hat by cutting small feather shapes from colored construction paper and gluing them in shapes.

- Have a hat parade!

Silhouettes

HISTORICAL AID:

Another form of paper art was the making of portrait silhouettes. The person to be captured in the artform was seated behind white paper. A candle was lit and placed behind the sitter whose profile was then cast onto the white paper. A machine was used which marked and reduced the shadow. The reduced silhouette was cut from black paper, mounted and framed.

Project:

Seat a child behind a piece of butcher paper. Shine a lamp behind the child so that a profile shadow is cast on the paper. Trace the shadow on to the paper.

Cut out the white paper outline and retrace it onto black paper. Then cut out this outline and mount the finished silhouette on white.

Fancy Initials

Project:
Design a fancy letter for the initial capital in your last name. Make several samples then select one for a final copy. Do this in either black ink or crayon. Your letter can be in printing or handwriting.

Cut Paper Art

HISTORICAL AID:

Decorative work known as *papyrotamia* involved the cutting of still paper into various shapes. These shapes were then put into designs and mounted on black paper, framed and glazed.

Intricate patterns were popular choices for the colonial artists. Valentines and wreaths were also themes.

Materials:
- Colored construction paper
- One sheet 12"x14" black construction paper
- Glue, scissors
- Clear spray lacquer

Project:

Decide on a theme for the artwork (see historical aid).

Cut the construction paper into the desired shapes and mount them with glue to the black paper.

Spray the finished artwork with clear lacquer to create a glazed effect.

Quilting

HISTORICAL AID:

For colonial women quilt making was not just the creation of a household item. Quilts were also a thrifty use of material fragments, a form of decoration and an expression of pride. Ladies exchanged intricately designed patterns each with its name such as Crow's Foot, Chinese Puzzle, Love-knot and Sunflower.

Groups of women would gather together for several days in quilting bees, working toward one result—the creation of a beautiful quilt.

Project:

• Supply each child with an 8″x8″ piece of white drawing paper.

• Using crayons, paint or paper scraps, decorate each square.

• Assemble the squares on the wall in a "quilt" for display.

Alternate Projects:

Older children may design their own intricate quilt patterns and give their design a name. Reproduce each pattern and make a quilt book. Students can color the patterns in their extra time.

Indian Corn

HISTORICAL AID

No one in England or Europe knew about corn so when the Pilgrims came to America they were introduced to this food by the Indians. The Indians grew all varieties of corn including those with red, blue, black and pink kernels. Corn was very colorful—some had bands, spots and stripes.

Materials:
Red, blue, black, yellow, pink tempera paint
White construction paper
Corn husks (available in grocery store produce sections)

Directions:
Dip your index finger into paint. Press the finger onto the white construction paper. Continue to "dip and press," making the shape of a corn cob. Select any colors and pattern you wish.

When the paint is dry, glue husks to each side of the corn cob.

Weathervane

Project:
Use the pattern on the next page or design your own. Trace the pattern onto cardboard and cut it out. Paint the cutout shape black on both sides. Glue it to a paint stirrer (obtainable from your local paint store). Put the bottom end of the paint stirrer into a clay base and "mount" it on your desk.

Weathervane Pattern

Silverware

The work of the silversmith was almost as important as that of blacksmiths. Their customers considered silverware an investment because the metal itself had a high value. Valuable silver pieces included candlesticks, platters, bowls , salt cellars and sets of tableware.

The skill of the silversmith could be seen in the intricate patterns engraved into the silverware.

Almost every colonial town had a silversmith but the main silversmithing centers were Boston, Philadelphia and New York City.

Project:
Cover a **sturdy paper plate** with **tin foil.**

Use a **toothpick** to carefully draw a design on the foil.

Toys

HISTORICAL AID

Children from wealthier families enjoyed dolls, tea sets and soldiers imported from England. But most colonial children played with home-made toys. These toys included balls, dolls, tops, marbles, whistles, kites, jump ropes and rolling hoops.

Project:
Experiment with top making. You can use spools, jar lids, cardboard, or any other round object in which you can punch a hole in the center. Push a stick, pencil, or nail through the hole. Which top can spin the longest? Older students can have a design contest. Younger students can work in groups with an adult to make their tops.

Other activities:
Spend an afternoon playing with colonial toys. Jump rope, fly kites and practice rolling hula hoops. Teach little fingers how to shoot a marble (excellent for small motor development). Older kids can make marble rolls in the sand or have shooting-for-accuracy contests.

All Dolled Up

HISTORICAL AID

Like their toys, the dolls of colonial children were usually homemade and very basic. Heads and bodies were shaped on a lathe with little hand carving. Limbs were little more than sticks. Clothes were patchworks of scraps from dressmaking or upholstery and glued directly onto the wooden bodies.

Dolls were also made from pine cones, cornhusks and rags. Dried apples were sometimes used for faces.

Spoon Doll
Materials:
Wooden ice cream spoon
Markers
Material scraps
Glue
Scissors

Directions:
Use markers to draw facial features on the rounded end of the spoon. Cut material scraps and glue clothing onto the spoon (see illustration).

Ragdoll

Materials:

One sock
Two rubber bands
Rags for stuffing
Glue, scissors
Buttons, ribbon, material

Directions:

Cut off an old sock just above the heel. Stuff the sock with rags.

Pull the bottom of the sock together and close with a rubber band.

To form the doll's neck, squeeze the sock a few inches from the end opposite the rubber band. Secure a rubber band over the section being squeezed to separate the head from the body.

Glue button eyes. Older children can glue material for clothing.

Children's Games

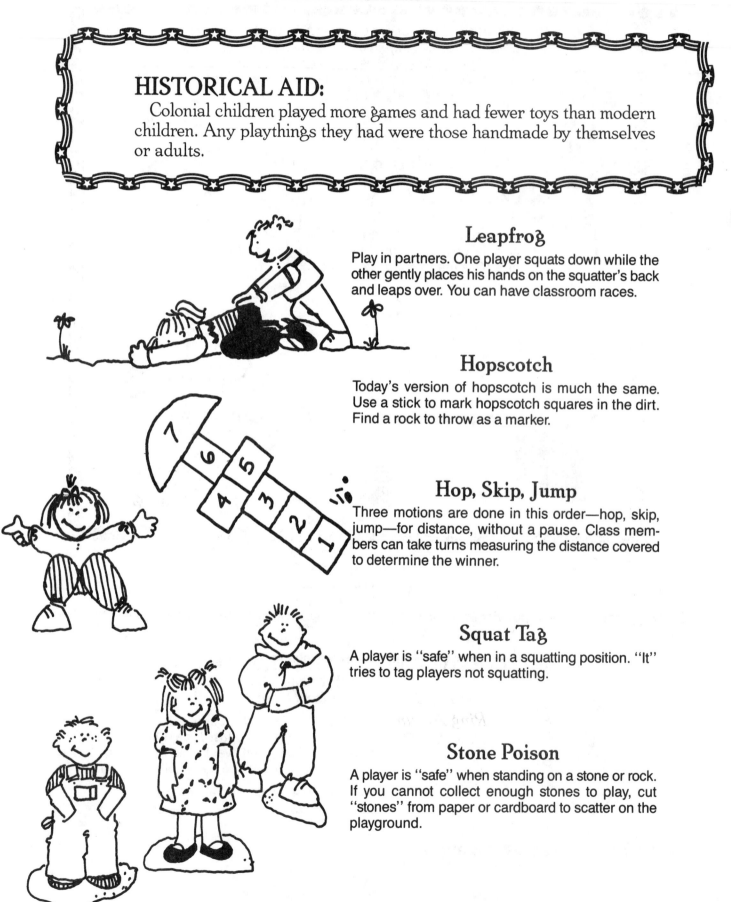

Leapfrog

Play in partners. One player squats down while the other gently places his hands on the squatter's back and leaps over. You can have classroom races.

Hopscotch

Today's version of hopscotch is much the same. Use a stick to mark hopscotch squares in the dirt. Find a rock to throw as a marker.

Hop, Skip, Jump

Three motions are done in this order—hop, skip, jump—for distance, without a pause. Class members can take turns measuring the distance covered to determine the winner.

Squat Tag

A player is "safe" when in a squatting position. "It" tries to tag players not squatting.

Stone Poison

A player is "safe" when standing on a stone or rock. If you cannot collect enough stones to play, cut "stones" from paper or cardboard to scatter on the playground.

Cat's Cradle

This game is also called cratch cradle. One player stretches a length of yarn over the extended fingers of both hands in a symmetrical form. The second player uses his fingers to remove the yarn without dropping the loops and tries to make another figure.

Bowling on the Grass

Set up empty milk cartons on the grass and roll a ball from a distance of about 15 feet. Try to knock over the cartons. Play on teams or individually, scoring a point each time a carton is hit. (Of course, colonial children did not have milk cartons and the nice balls that children of today do!)

Singing games were also popular. You will recognize these games are still being played today. Here are some to try:

London Bridge is Falling Down
Ring Around a Rosy
Here We Go Round the Mulberry Bush

Other recognizable colonial games to play:

Marbles
Blindman's Bluff

Hornbook

HISTORICAL AID:

The first book from which the colonial children learned was not really a book at all. It was a thin piece of wood about five inches long with a handle. This wood was covered with a thin piece of paper attached around the edges with a thin sheet of clear horn. The handle had a hole through which string was strung. The hornbook was worn around the neck or hung by the side.

On the paper was printed the alphabet, alphabet letter combinations (such as *eb*, *ib*, *ob*), Lord's Prayer and Roman numerals.

Materials
Pattern reproduced from following page
Cardboard
Glue
Yarn

Directions
Cut out hornbook pattern.

Trace the pattern onto cardboard.

Cut out the cardboard pattern.

Print the alphabet, numbers, Roman numerals, etc., on the paper hornbook.

Glue the paper to the cardboard.

Punch a hole in the handle and tie with yarn to fit around the neck.

Hornbook Pattern

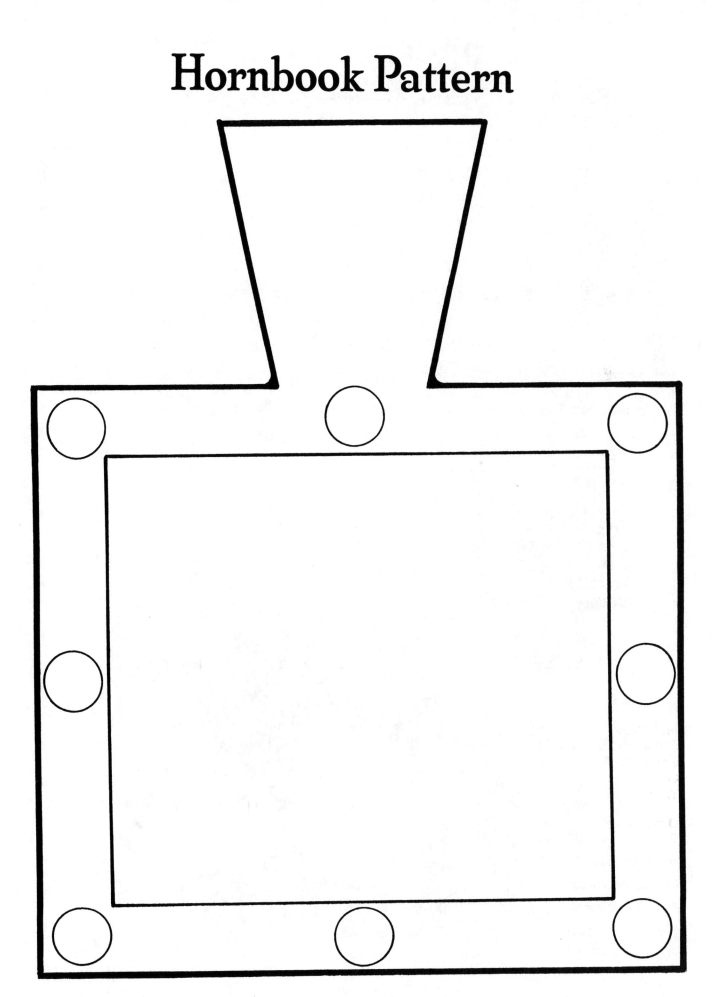

Gingerbread Letters

HISTORICAL AID:

The colonists brought with them to their new world the tradition of making hornbooks (see previous page) from gingerbread. Housewives would cut letters from gingerbread or use cookie molds to make these edible treats that were sometimes sold and also used as a reward for learning a letter.

Directions

Make gingerbread using a packaged mix.

Instead of using a deep pan spread the batter on a prepared cookie sheet. Bake until a knife inserted comes out clean. The time will be reduced from that indicated on the package.

Using a knife, cut the gingerbread into an alphabet letter.

Enjoy!

Quill

HISTORICAL AID

Pens for writing were hand cut from the quill (feather) of a goose or wild turkey. The tips were sharpened with a knife. The sharp tips were then dipped into ink for writing. Only a few symbols could be written before the quill needed to be dipped again. Writing with a quill was a very time consuming task!

Project:

Reproduce the pattern below. Sponge paint with bright colors. Cut out the dried feather. Glue a toothpick to the pointed end. Try dipping the pen into ink (homemade or store bought) and writing on paper.

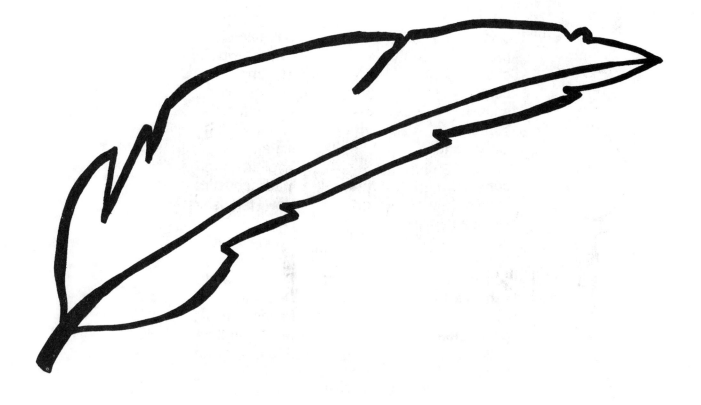

Spelling Bee

HISTORICAL AID:

The children of rich colonists attended private schools or were educated by private teachers called *tutors*. New England had many private schools called *dame* schools. Women, often widows, held these schools in their own homes. Church groups also operated schools. The ministers held classes in their homes.

Children were taught the alphabet, spelling, writing and simple arithmetic. Most of the children paid fees for their education.

One of the activities the children enjoyed was a *spelling bee*. Children of today still participate in this activity in their classrooms.

Activity

Reproduce the list of colonial-related words for the children to study. Then have a Spelling Bee.

colony	Squanto
pumpkin	Jamestown
charter	Pilgrim
corn	Mayflower
squash	Plymouth
hornbook	Thanksgiving
settlement	Indian
turkey	Virginia
compact	Massachusetts
candle	New Hampshire
almanac	New York
barter	Connecticut
harvest	Maryland
succotash	Rhode Island
ashcake	Delaware
quilt	Pennsylvania
gingerbread	North Carolina
quill	South Carolina
postrider	Georgia

Apprenticeship

Activity

Set up an apprentice system in your classroom. Everyone has something they can teach or show the rest of the class. Discuss with the children what skill they might share (sport, game, art, cooking etc.).

Assign partners. One is the craftsman, one is the apprentice. The craftsman will teach the apprentice. Then change roles. Assign new partners and repeat the process.

The amount of time an apprentice spends with his or her teacher will depend on the age of the children and the skills being taught and shared.

Almanac Adventures

HISTORICAL AID:

One of the most popular and influential works printed in colonial America was *Poor Richard's Almanac*. Written and published by Benjamin Franklin, the book was issued every year from 1733 to 1758.

Poor Richard's Almanac featured practical advice, poems, jokes, weather predictions and proverbs. Such well-known proverbs as "A penny saved is a penny earned" and "Early to bed, early to rise makes a man healthy, wealthy and wise" were found in the almanac.

Projects:

• Create a classroom of individual almanacs. Provide each child with two pieces of paper. Fold in half to make booklet size. Label the four resulting pages **Advice**, **Jokes**, **Poems**, and **Proverbs**. Fill in the pages with appropriate information, either of the students' creation or gathered from resources.

• Assemble the finished pages and staple on a cover.